Sanjeev Kapoor

Home Makers' DELIGHT

Vegetarian Recipes for Everyday Cooking

In association with Alyona Kapoor

Popular Prakashan
www.popularprakashan.com

Published by
POPULAR PRAKASHAN PVT. LTD.
301, Mahalaxmi Chambers
22, Bhulabhai Desai Road
Mumbai - 400 026
for KHANA KHAZANA PUBLICATIONS PVT. LTD.

First Published 2015

(4279)
ISBN: 978-81-7991-531-8

Design: Anjali Sawant
Photography: Sumeet Ballal

PRINTED IN INDIA
by Saurabh Printers (P) Ltd.
Plot No. 67 A-68, Ecotech, Ext. I
Kasna, Greater Noida-201306 (U.P)

Author's Note

During the interactive sessions after every live cookery demonstration, I had scores of housewives coming up to me and saying, "Chef, it is so much easier to plan the menu for parties but we find it so difficult to decide what to cook every day. Why don't you come up with a book of recipes that are suitable for everyday cooking?" I could understand their problem, since we also experience the same thing at home.

In *Home Makers' Delight - Vegetarian Recipes for Everyday Cooking* I have compiled recipes that are healthy, tasty, and easy to make any day of the week. Use this ready reckoner and serve delicious and nutritious meals to your loved ones. All the recipes in the book are meant for four portions, keeping in mind that they form a part of a menu with other dishes to complement them.

Happy cooking!

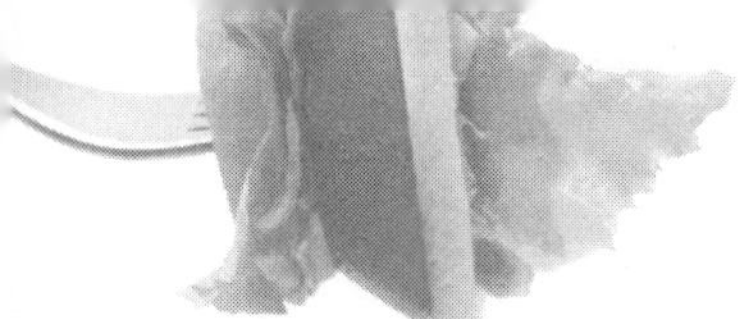

CONTENTS

Snacks and Breakfast

Buttermilk Pancake 6

Rice Vermicelli Upma with South Indian Coffee 7

Bread Pakora with Chhunda 11

Tomato and Onion Omelette 13

Sooji Pancake 14

Sanja 16

Karele ke Chilke ke Pakore 17

Corn and Pesto Mini Pizza 21

Soups and Salads

Paushtik Tomato Soup 22

Cheesy Mushroom Coriander Soup 24

Andhra Pepper Rasam 25

Tangy Carrot Soup 27

Sprouts and Apple Salad 31

Week Days

Cauliflower Paneer Bhurji 32

Cabbage Sambhariya 33

Tamatar aur Moongphalli ki Sabzi 34

Soya Matar Bhurji 35

Gavar Phalli Aloo ki Sabzi 36

Kaaley Masalewale Aloo 38

Batatachya Kachrya 41

Lal Maat ki Sabzi 42

Rajasthani Kaddu ki Sabzi 43

Sing no Lotwalo Shaak 44

Doodhi Thepla and Spicy

Garlic Chutney 46
Besan Karela 47
Matar Pyaazwale 51
Tamarind Rice 52
Aloo Chutney Pulao 54
Wadi aur Matar Pulao 55
Pyaaz aur Pudine ki Roti 57

Weekend Special

Spicy Pinwheels 58
Idli Fry 61
Spicy Moong Dal Dhokla 62
Dal Dhokli 63
Fansi Dhokli 65
Rajma Cheese Parantha 67
Spicy Red Mexican Rice 71
Chana Dal Halwa 72
Palak Methi Puri 73
Bajre ke Bharwan Paranthe 74
Hara Bhara Paneer 76
Sweetcorn and Capsicum Stir-Fry 77
Papad Koshimbir 79

Quick Cooking

Carrot Methi Sabzi 80
Kurkuri Ajwaini Bhindi 81
Pressure-Cooked Aloo Sabzi 82
Hare Moong ki Chhaaswali Khichdi 83
Bhein Masala 84
Tender Coconut and Sago Kheer 86
Nariyal ka Halwa 89
Quick Trifle 90
Sooji aur Badam ka Halwa 91
Mango Cheesecake 92

Basic recipes 94

Glossary 95

Buttermilk Pancake

- 1 cup buttermilk
- 1 cup refined flour
- 1 teaspoon baking powder
- ½ teaspoon soda bicarbonate
- ¼ teaspoon salt
- 4 tablespoons oil
- ½ teaspoon mustard seeds
- 10-12 curry leaves, chopped
- ½ inch ginger, chopped
- 1 green chilli, chopped

1. Combine the flour, baking powder, soda bicarbonate and salt in a bowl.
2. In another bowl, combine the buttermilk and three tablespoons of oil and mix well. Add to the flour mixture and stir quickly until well blended, taking care that there are no lumps.
3. Heat the remaining oil in a non-stick pan. Add the mustard seeds, curry leaves, ginger and green chilli and sauté till the mustard seeds splutter. Add to the mixture and mix well. Heat a non-stick tawa. Pour and spread a ladleful of the mixture to make a thick pancake. Cook for two to three minutes on each side. Serve hot.

Rice Vermicelli Upma with South Indian Coffee

2 cups rice vermicelli
2 tablespoons oil
½ teaspoon mustard seeds
1 teaspoon cumin seeds
1 teaspoon skinless split black gram
2 green chillies, slit
8-10 curry leaves
A pinch of asafoetida
1 large onion, finely chopped
1 large tomato, finely chopped
¼ cup shelled green peas
Salt to taste
2 tablespoons chopped fresh coriander

1. Dry-roast the rice vermicelli in a non-stick pan till brown. Transfer to a bowl and set aside.
2. Heat the oil in the same pan. Add the mustard seeds and let them splutter. Add the cumin seeds, black gram, green chillies, curry leaves and asafoetida.

3. Mix well and add the onion and sauté till onion turns brown. Add the tomato and sauté for half a minute. Add the green peas and mix well. Cook for two to three minutes.
4. Add the salt and roasted rice vermicelli and mix well. Add four cups of hot water. Mix well, cover and cook till the vermicelli is done. Garnish with the chopped coriander and serve hot.

South Indian Coffee

9 tablespoons finely ground dark roasted coffee powder

3 cups milk

¼ cup granulated sugar

1. Place the coffee powder in a filter over a coffeepot. Pour in one cup of boiling water. When the first cup has completely soaked through, pour in the second cup.
2. Since the powder is very fine, it will take a few minutes for water to drip through.
3. While coffee is dripping through, heat the milk and sugar in a non-stick pan until very hot but not boiling.
4. Add the milk to the brewed coffee decoction and serve hot.

South Indian Coffee
Rice Vermicelli Upma

Bread Pakora with Chhunda

Tomato and Onion Omelette

Bread Pakora with Chhunda

8 white bread slices
8 tablespoons chhunda
1½ cups gram flour
¼ teaspoon turmeric powder
1 teaspoon red chilli powder
½ teaspoon carom seeds
Salt to taste
A pinch of soda bicarbonate
2-3 tablespoons rice flour
2 tablespoons chopped fresh coriander
Oil for deep-frying
2 teaspoons Chaat Masala (page 94)

1. Arrange four bread slices on a flat surface and spread two tablespoons of chhunda on each of them.
2. Cover them with the remaining slices and cut each into four triangles.
3. Combine the gram flour, turmeric powder, chilli powder, carom seeds, salt, soda bicarbonate, rice flour and chopped coriander in a bowl.

4. Add water, little by little, and mix well to make a smooth and lump-free batter.
5. Heat sufficient oil in a kadai. Dip each bread triangle in the batter and slide it into the hot oil.
6. Deep-fry till golden brown and crisp on both sides. Drain on absorbent paper.
7. Sprinkle the chaat masala on them and serve hot.

Chef's Note: Chhunda is a sweet and spicy grated mango pickle of Gujarat.

Tomato and Onion Omelette

1 large tomato, chopped
1 large onion, chopped
4 eggs
2 tablespoons butter
1 green chilli, chopped
¼ teaspoon ginger paste
¼ teaspoon garlic paste
Salt to taste
¼ teaspoon red chilli powder

1. Heat the butter in a non-stick pan. Add the onion and sauté till soft.
2. Add the green chilli, ginger paste, garlic paste and sauté for a minute. Add the tomato and cook for two to three minutes. Add the salt, chilli powder and mix.
3. Whisk the eggs in a separate bowl and add it to the onion and tomato mixture. Mix well. Cover the pan and cook till the eggs are set. Flip once to cook the other side.
4. Cut into wedges and serve hot with brown bread slices.

(Image on page 10)

Sooji Pancake

1 cup coarse semolina	6 tablespoons yogurt
¼ cup gram flour	¼ teaspoon fruit salt
Salt to taste	Oil for shallow-frying
½ teaspoon cumin seeds	1 medium tomato, finely chopped
A pinch of asafoetida	100 grams processed cheese, grated
2 green chillies, chopped	2 tablespoons chopped fresh coriander

1. Combine the semolina, gram flour, salt, cumin seeds, asafoetida, green chillies, yogurt and sufficient water to make a smooth batter.
2. Let it rest for fifteen to twenty minutes.
3. Add the fruit salt to the batter and mix.
4. Heat a non-stick pan. Drizzle a little oil on the pan, spread a ladleful of batter to make a four-inch thick pancake.

5. Cook on medium heat. Sprinkle the tomato, cheese and the chopped coriander over it. Cover and cook for three to four minutes.
6. Uncover the pan and drizzle a little oil all around and cook till the underside is crisp.
7. Serve hot.

Sanja

- 1 cup coarse semolina, roasted
- 2 tablespoons oil
- 1 teaspoon mustard seeds
- 1 teaspoon cumin seeds
- A pinch of asafoetida
- 5-6 curry leaves
- 3 medium onions, chopped
- 3 green chillies, chopped
- ½ teaspoon turmeric powder
- Salt to taste
- 4 tablespoons chopped fresh coriander
- 4 tablespoons grated fresh coconut

1. Heat the oil in a deep non-stick pan.
2. Add the mustard seeds and cumin seeds. When they begin to splutter, add the asafoetida, curry leaves, onions and cook till the onions are soft.
3. Add the green chillies, turmeric powder, salt and mix. Add the roasted semolina and mix.

4. Add two and a half cups of hot water and cover the pan. Cook on low heat for about five or six minutes.
5. Garnish with the chopped coriander and grated coconut and serve hot.

Chef's Tip

Semolina should be roasted over moderate heat. Stir it continuously to prevent over-roasting.

Karele ke Chilke ke Pakore

20 bitter gourds
1 cup gram flour
Salt to taste
1 teaspoon turmeric powder
Oil for deep-frying
2 teaspoons coriander powder

1 teaspoon carom seeds | 1 teaspoon cumin powder
1 teaspoon red chilli powder | A large pinch of Chaat Masala (page 94)

1. Peel the bitter gourds and reserve the skin.
2. Sprinkle a little salt and turmeric powder on the skin and set aside for ten to fifteen minutes. Heat sufficient oil in a kadai.
3. Squeeze out the excess juice from the bitter gourd skin and transfer into a bowl. Add the coriander powder, carom seeds, chilli powder, cumin powder, salt and gram flour and mix well. Add five tablespoons of water to make a thick, smooth batter.
4. Moisten the palm of your hand; take small portions of the mixture and slide them into the hot oil.
5. Deep-fry the pakore till half done and drain on absorbent paper. Reheat the oil. Deep-fry the pakore again till golden and crisp. Drain on absorbent paper.
6. Sprinkle the chaat masala. Transfer onto a serving plate and serve hot.

Karele ke Chilke ke Pakore

Corn and Pesto Mini Pizza

Corn and Pesto Mini Pizza

1 cup American corn kernels, blanched and crushed

8 mini pizza breads

Pesto Sauce

30-40 (¾ cup) fresh basil

3-4 garlic cloves

Salt to taste

1 tablespoon pine nuts

6 tablespoons olive oil

4-5 black peppercorns

¼ cup Parmesan cheese

Topping

8 tablespoons grated mozzarella cheese

Dried oregano and red chilli flakes, for sprinkling

1. Preheat an oven to 180°C/350°F/Gas Mark 4.
2. Arrange the pizza breads on the tray and bake for eight to ten minutes or till slightly crisp.

3. To make the pesto sauce, grind the fresh basil, garlic and salt in a blender.
4. Add the pine nuts, olive oil, peppercorns and Parmesan cheese, one after the other, and grind till all the ingredients are well mixed. Transfer into a bowl.
5. Spread the pesto sauce on top of the pizza breads. Sprinkle the crushed corn over this. Sprinkle one tablespoon of mozzarella cheese on each pizza and bake for five to six minutes, or till the cheese melts.
6. Remove from the oven and sprinkle the oregano and red chilli flakes. Serve hot.

Paushtik Tomato Soup

6 medium tomatoes, roughly chopped	1 large onion, roughly chopped
1 teaspoon butter	Salt to taste
4-5 garlic cloves, crushed	¼ cup skinless split green gram, soaked

5-6 fresh coriander stems, roughly chopped

Black pepper powder to taste

¼ cup bean sprouts, for garnishing

1. Heat the butter in a pressure cooker.
2. Add the garlic and onion and sauté till the onion is translucent.
3. Add the tomatoes, salt, split green gram, coriander stems and two cups of water. Mix and bring it to a boil.
4. Cover and cook under pressure till the pressure is released five times (five whistles). Open the lid once the pressure has completely reduced. Transfer the mixture into a blender jar and blend into a smooth purée.
5. Pour the purée into a deep non-stick pan and bring it to a boil.
6. Adjust the salt and add black pepper powder. Garnish with the bean sprouts and serve hot.

Cheesy Mushroom Coriander Soup

½ cup grated cheese

200 grams fresh button mushrooms, sliced

½ cup chopped fresh coriander

100 grams fresh coriander roots

3 tablespoons butter

2 medium onions, chopped

6-8 garlic cloves, chopped

A pinch of nutmeg powder

2 cups milk

Salt to taste

Black pepper powder to taste

1. Heat two tablespoons butter in a non-stick pan.
2. Add the onions, garlic and coriander roots and sauté till onions become translucent.
3. Add the mushrooms and nutmeg powder and sauté for five to eight minutes. Add the chopped coriander and sauté for one minute.
4. Add four cups of water and bring to a boil.

5. Simmer till it is reduced to half its original volume. Discard the coriander roots and transfer into a blender jar.
6. Blend till smooth. Transfer into a deep non-stick pan and add the milk gradually, stirring continuously. Boil the soup for three to four minutes.
7. Add the salt, pepper powder and remaining butter and mix well. Sprinkle the cheese and serve piping hot.

Andhra Pepper Rasam

4 tablespoons split pigeon peas, boiled

1 medium tomato, chopped

¼ teaspoon turmeric powder

Salt to taste

1 tablespoon Tamarind Pulp (page 94)

½ teaspoon red chilli powder

2 tablespoons chopped fresh coriander

Rasam Powder	Seasoning
20-25 black peppercorns	2 tablespoons oil
1 tablespoon coriander seeds	½ teaspoon mustard seeds
1 teaspoon cumin seeds	¼ teaspoon asafoetida
A pinch of fenugreek seeds	2 dried red chillies, broken
1 tablespoon split pigeon peas	8-10 curry leaves
	2 teaspoons black pepper powder

1. To make the rasam powder, dry-roast the coriander seeds, cumin seeds, fenugreek seeds, pigeon peas and peppercorns till fragrant. Cool and grind to a fine powder.
2. Strain the boiled dal and put into a deep non-stick pan and mash well. Add the water in which it was cooked and mix.
3. Add the tomato, turmeric powder, salt, tamarind pulp, chilli powder, three tablespoons of prepared rasam powder and mix well. Add three cups of water and cook till the mixture reduces to half its original volume.

4. To make the seasoning, heat the oil in a small non-stick pan. Add the mustard seeds. Once they splutter, add the asafoetida, red chillies, curry leaves and pepper powder. Pour this seasoning over the prepared rasam. Cover the pan to trap the flavours.

5. Serve hot, garnished with the chopped coriander.

Tangy Carrot Soup

250 grams carrots, chopped
1 teaspoon butter
1 medium onion, chopped
8-10 black peppercorns
1 inch ginger, chopped
1 medium potato, chopped
4 cups Vegetable Stock (page 94)
2 tablespoons chopped fresh coriander
Salt to taste
¼ teaspoon black pepper powder

1. Heat the butter in a deep non-stick pan. Add the onion, peppercorns and ginger. Sauté for two minutes or till onion changes colour.
2. Add the carrots and potato and sauté on low heat for two to three minutes. Add two cups of the vegetable stock and bring it to a boil.
3. Cover and cook for ten to fifteen minutes or till the vegetables are cooked.
4. Cool, transfer into a blender jar and blend it to a purée.
5. Strain the vegetable purée into a deep non-stick pan. Add the remaining vegetable stock and bring it to a boil.
6. Add the chopped coriander, salt and pepper powder. Mix well.
7. Serve hot.

Tangy Carrot Soup

Sprouts and Apple Salad

Sprouts and Apple Salad

1½ cups bean sprouts, blanched

2 apples

6-8 iceberg lettuce

1 medium onion, sliced

1 medium tomato, chopped

For dressing

2 tablespoons olive oil

¼ cup apple juice

1 tablespoon lemon juice

½ teaspoon black pepper powder

½ teaspoon mustard paste

Salt to taste

1. Wash and soak the lettuce leaves in ice-cold water for about fifteen minutes.
2. To make the dressing, put the olive oil, apple juice, lemon juice, pepper powder, mustard paste and salt in a small bowl and whisk well. Set aside. Chop the apples into small pieces. Place them with the sprouts, onion, and tomato in a large bowl.
3. Drain the lettuce, tear them into bite-sized pieces, and add them to the sprout mixture and toss. Pour the dressing on the salad and toss lightly. Serve immediately.

Cauliflower Paneer Bhurji

2 cups grated cauliflower
2 cups crumbled cottage cheese
2 tablespoons oil
1 teaspoon cumin seeds
1 inch ginger, chopped
2 green chillies, chopped
2 medium onions, chopped
2 medium tomatoes, chopped
1 teaspoon turmeric powder
2 teaspoons red chilli powder
Salt to taste
2 tablespoons chopped fresh coriander

1. Heat the oil in a non-stick pan; add the cumin seeds, ginger, green chillies and sauté for a minute.
2. Add the onions and sauté till the onions become translucent. Add the tomatoes and cook till soft. Add the turmeric powder, chilli powder and salt and sauté for a minute.
3. Add the cauliflower and cottage cheese. Mix well and cook till the cauliflower is done. Garnish with chopped coriander and serve hot.

Cabbage Sambhariya

200 grams cabbage, shredded
1 tablespoon oil
½ teaspoon mustard seeds
2 green chillies, slit
A pinch of asafoetida
½ teaspoon turmeric powder
1 medium green capsicum, cut into small pieces
Salt to taste

1. Heat the oil in a non-stick kadai; add the mustard seeds and let them splutter. Add the green chillies and sauté for half a minute.
2. Add the asafoetida and turmeric powder and mix. Add the capsicum and sauté for a minute.
3. Add the cabbage and salt and mix. Cover and cook for seven to eight minutes. Uncover and stir lightly.
4. Serve hot or cold.

Tamatar aur Moongphalli ki Sabzi

8 large tomatoes, finely chopped

8 tablespoons roasted and crushed peanuts

2 tablespoons oil

1 teaspoon mustard seeds

¼ teaspoon asafoetida

8-10 curry leaves

2 green chillies, chopped

¼ teaspoon turmeric powder

1 teaspoon red chilli powder

Salt to taste

2 teaspoons sugar

¼ cup chopped fresh coriander

1. Heat the oil in a non-stick pan. Add the mustard seeds. As they begin to splutter, add the asafoetida, curry leaves and green chillies and sauté for thirty seconds.
2. Add the tomatoes, turmeric powder, chilli powder, salt, sugar and sauté for five to six minutes or till the tomatoes are soft.
3. Add the peanuts, chopped coriander and half cup of water. Stir and bring to a boil. Serve hot.

Soya Matar Bhurji

300 grams soya nuggets, soaked
1 cup shelled green peas
1½ teaspoons oil
1 teaspoon cumin seeds
2 medium onions, finely chopped
1 inch ginger, finely chopped
2 green chillies, finely chopped
½ teaspoon turmeric powder
1 teaspoon cumin powder
1 tablespoon coriander powder
1 teaspoon red chilli powder
1 medium tomato, finely chopped
1 medium green capsicum, finely chopped
Salt to taste
2 tablespoons chopped fresh coriander

1. Drain the soya nuggets and then crumble them into smaller pieces. Heat the oil in a non-stick pan.
2. Add the cumin seeds and when they begin to change colour, add the onions, ginger and green chillies. Sauté till the onions become translucent.

3. Mix the turmeric powder, cumin powder, coriander powder and chilli powder with half cup of water and add to the pan. Cook on medium heat for half a minute, stirring continuously.
4. Add the tomato and cook on high heat for two minutes, stirring continuously. Stir in the crumbled soya nuggets, green peas, capsicum, and salt. Mix well.
5. Reduce the heat and cook for two to three minutes, stirring frequently to prevent sticking. Sprinkle the chopped coriander on top and serve hot.

Gavar Phalli Aloo ki Sabzi

250 grams cluster beans, stringed and trimmed at both ends

2 medium potatoes, quartered

3 tablespoons oil

½ teaspoon mustard seeds

½ teaspoon cumin seeds

½ teaspoon carom seeds

A pinch of asafoetida	1 tablespoon coriander-cumin powder
1 medium onion, chopped	Salt to taste
½ teaspoon turmeric powder	2 tablespoons grated jaggery
¾ teaspoon red chilli powder	1 teaspoon dried mango powder

1. Break the cluster beans into two to three pieces each or cut them into one-inch pieces.
2. Heat the oil in a deep non-stick kadai and add the mustard seeds. As they begin to splutter, add the cumin seeds, carom seeds and asafoetida.
3. Add the onion and sauté till golden brown. Add the cluster beans and potatoes and stir well. Add three to four tablespoons of water and mix.
4. Cover and cook on low heat, stirring occasionally, till cluster beans are half cooked.
5. Add the turmeric powder, chilli powder, coriander-cumin powder and salt.
6. Stir well and cook till done. Add the jaggery and dried mango powder and mix well. Cook till well blended. Serve hot with rotli.

(Image on page 39)

Kaaley Masalewale Aloo

6-8 medium potatoes, boiled, peeled and cubed

2 tablespoons ghee

1 teaspoon cumin seeds

½ teaspoon onion seeds

½ teaspoon black mustard seeds

¼ teaspoon black salt

Salt to taste

1½ teaspoons crushed black peppercorns

1½ teaspoons roasted cumin powder

1 teaspoon black sesame seeds

½ teaspoon Garam Masala Powder (page 94)

2 teaspoons dried mango powder

1. Heat the ghee in a non-stick kadai; add the cumin seeds, onion seeds and black mustard seeds. When the seeds splutter, add the potatoes and stir well.
2. Add the black salt, salt, crushed peppercorns, cumin powder and sesame seeds and mix well. Cover and cook for three to four minutes.
3. Add the garam masala powder and dried mango powder and mix lightly. Serve hot.

Kaaley Masalewale Aloo

Gavar Phalli Aloo ki Sabzi

Batatachya Kachrya

Batatachya Kachrya

6 medium potatoes
3 tablespoons oil
½ teaspoon mustard seeds
½ teaspoon cumin seeds
A pinch of asafoetida
Salt to taste
½ teaspoon turmeric powder
¼ teaspoon red chilli powder
4 tablespoons chopped fresh coriander

1. Peel the potatoes, quarter lengthwise, and then cut into thin slices.
2. Heat the oil in a deep non-stick kadai. Add the mustard seeds and as they begin to splutter, add the cumin seeds. As they begin to change colour, add the asafoetida and potatoes and mix well.
3. Add the turmeric powder and chilli powder and mix well. Sprinkle a little water and cover the kadai. Cook on medium-low heat, stirring occasionally, till done. Add the chopped coriander and mix well. Serve hot with roti.

Chef's Note Batata is the Marathi word for potato.

Lal Maat ki Sabzi

500 grams red amaranth leaves, chopped
2 teaspoons oil
5-6 garlic cloves, crushed
2 green chillies, halved
2 large onions, chopped
Sea salt to taste

1. Heat the oil in a non-stick pan; add the garlic and sauté till light brown.
2. Add the green chillies and onions and sauté till the onions are golden brown.
3. Add the salt and mix well and sauté for a minute. Add the amaranth leaves and cook for five to eight minutes or till the leaves reduce in size.
4. Serve hot with rice bhakri.

Chef's Note Laal Maat is the Marathi word for red amaranth.

Rajasthani Kaddu ki Sabzi

250 grams pumpkin, cut into 1-inch cubes with skin

1 large potato, cut into 1-inch cubes

2 tablespoons oil

½ teaspoon cumin seeds

½ teaspoon asafoetida

¼ teaspoon turmeric powder

1 teaspoon red chilli powder

1 tablespoon coriander powder

½ teaspoon dried mango powder

¼ teaspoon Garam Masala Powder (page 94)

Salt to taste

2 tablespoons chopped fresh coriander

1. Heat the oil in a non-stick pan. Add the cumin seeds, asafoetida and turmeric powder. When the seeds begin to change colour add the potato and cook for one to two minutes.
2. Add the pumpkin and mix well. Add the chilli powder, coriander powder, dried mango powder and mix well.

3. Add one-fourth cup of water, cover and cook for four to five minutes or till the vegetables are almost tender.
4. Add the garam masala powder and salt and mix.
5. Cover and cook for five to seven minutes or till the vegetables are completely cooked and soft.
6. Serve hot, garnished with the chopped coriander.

Sing no Lotwalo Shaak

3 drumsticks (sing), cut into 4-inch pieces

2 tablespoons gram flour

3 tablespoons oil

½ teaspoon mustard seeds

½ teaspoon cumin seeds

¼ teaspoon asafoetida

Salt to taste

3 medium potatoes, chopped

1 cup yogurt

2 teaspoons sugar ½ teaspoon red chilli powder

¼ teaspoon turmeric powder 1 tablespoon chopped fresh coriander

1. Heat the oil in a non-stick pan. Add the mustard seeds and when they splutter, add the cumin seeds, asafoetida, drumsticks, salt and potatoes and mix well.
2. Add one and a half cups of water and let it cook for five to seven minutes or till drumsticks and potatoes are tender.
3. In a bowl, whisk yogurt and gram flour together.
4. Add the sugar, turmeric powder, chilli powder and whisk till the sugar is dissolved and no lumps remain. Add the yogurt mixture to the cooked drumsticks.
5. Cook, stirring, till gravy thickens. Garnish with the chopped coriander and serve hot.

Chef's Note: 1) Make sure that the yogurt is not sour.
2) Lot means 'flour' in Gujarati; in this recipe we use gram flour.
3) Sing is Gujarati word for drumsticks.

Doodhi Thepla and Spicy Garlic Chutney

- 1 cup grated bottle gourd
- 2 cups whole-wheat flour
- ½ cup yogurt
- Salt to taste
- 1 teaspoon cumin seeds
- ½ teaspoon turmeric powder
- 1 teaspoon red chilli powder
- ½ tablespoon coriander powder
- 2 tablespoons oil + for shallow-frying

1. Squeeze the grated bottle gourd to remove excess juice and reserve the juice.
2. Place the bottle gourd in a deep bowl. Add the flour, yogurt, salt, cumin seeds, turmeric powder, chilli powder, coriander powder and two tablespoons of oil.
3. Knead into a soft dough, using the reserved juice as required. Cover with a damp piece of muslin and rest it for ten to fifteen minutes.
4. Divide into sixteen equal portions and shape into balls. Roll out each ball into a thin thepla.

5. Heat a non-stick tawa and shallow-fry each thepla, applying a little oil on either side, till both sides are evenly golden. Serve hot.

Chef's Note Doodhi is Marathi word for bottle gouard.

Spicy Garlic Chutney

In a non-stick pan; boil 10 dried Kashmiri chillies, seeded; 8 large garlic cloves and ½ cup vinegar for six to eight minutes or till soft. Drain, cool, and grind into a smooth paste. Transfer into a bowl. Add the sea salt to taste, 2 teaspoons lemon juice and 1 teaspoon cumin powder. Mix well and serve.

Besan Karela

3 tablespoons gram flour

3 medium bitter gourds, lightly scraped

Salt to taste

5 tablespoons oil

¼ teaspoon asafoetida

½ teaspoon carom seeds

½ teaspoon dried mango powder

¾ teaspoon turmeric powder
1 teaspoon red chilli powder
2 teaspoons coriander-cumin powder
3 teaspoons sugar
1 tablespoon chopped fresh coriander

1. Chop the bitter gourds into small cubes. Sprinkle a little salt and mix. Set aside for thirty minutes. Squeeze out excess juices.
2. Heat the oil in a non-stick kadai and add the bitter gourds. Sauté on medium heat till lightly coloured. Cover and cook till done.
3. Sprinkle the gram flour and toss well.
4. Add the carom seeds, dried mango powder, turmeric powder, chilli powder, coriander-cumin powder and sugar and toss again. Continue to cook on medium-low heat, sprinkling a little water occasionally.
5. Cook till the gram flour coats the bitter gourds well.
6. Adjust salt. Take the kadai off the heat and serve garnished with the chopped coriander.

Besan Karela

Matar Pyaazwale

Matar Pyaazwale

- 2 cups shelled green peas, boiled
- 3 medium onions, cut into rings
- 2 medium tomatoes
- 2 teaspoons oil
- 1 teaspoon cumin seeds
- ½ inch ginger, finely chopped
- 1 teaspoon red chilli powder
- 2 teaspoon coriander-cumin powder
- ¾ teaspoon Garam Masala Powder (page 94)
- ½ teaspoon dried mango powder
- Salt to taste
- ¼ cup chopped fresh coriander

1. Boil two cups of water in a deep non-stick pan. Add the tomatoes and remove after three to four minutes.
2. Cool a little; peel and blend into a smooth purée. Set aside.
3. Heat the oil in a non-stick pan. Add the cumin seeds and when the seeds begin to change colour, add the onion rings and sauté till they are light brown.

4. Add the ginger and sauté for two minutes. Add the tomato purée, chilli powder, coriander-cumin powder, garam masala powder and dried mango powder. Mix well and cook for seven to eight minutes. Sprinkle two tablespoons of water.
5. Add the green peas and salt. Mix well and cook for one to two minutes.
6. Serve hot, garnished with the chopped coriander.

Tamarind Rice

3 tablespoons Tamarind Pulp (page 94)
2 cups cooked rice
3 tablespoons oil
4 dried red chillies, broken in half
1 teaspoon mustard seeds
2 tablespoons split Bengal gram
2 tablespoons split skinless black gram
10-12 curry leaves

¼ cup roasted peanuts
½ teaspoon sugar
Salt to taste
1 tablespoon chopped fresh coriander

1. Heat two tablespoons of oil in a deep non-stick pan; add the dried red chillies, mustard seeds, Bengal gram and black gram.
2. Sauté for two to three minutes or till the gram become brown in colour.
3. Add the curry leaves, roasted peanuts and sauté for half a minute.
4. Add the tamarind pulp, salt and sugar and cook for two to three minutes.
5. Add the rice and mix well. Stir and cover the pan tightly and let it steam for a few minutes. Garnish with the chopped coriander.
6. Serve hot.

Aloo Chutney Pulao

2 medium potatoes, cut into ½-inch pieces

6 tablespoons Green Chutney (page 94)

1½ cups Basmati rice, soaked for ½ hour and drained

2 tablespoons oil

1 bay leaf

2 black cardamoms

3-4 green cardamoms

3-4 cloves

1 inch cinnamon

4 black peppercorns

2 medium onions, sliced

3½ tablespoons spinach purée

Salt to taste

1. Heat the oil in a non-stick pan. Add the bay leaf, black cardamoms, green cardamoms, cloves, cinnamon, and peppercorns and sauté for a minute.

2. Add the onions and sauté till light brown.
3. Add the potatoes and mix. Add the spinach purée, green chutney, rice, three cups of water and salt and mix well.
4. Allow the mixture to come to a boil. Cover and cook on low heat for ten minutes.
5. Take the pan off the heat and let it stand for five more minutes.
6. Serve hot.

Wadi aur Matar Pulao

5-6 skinless split black gram nuggets, roughly crushed	1½ cups Basmati rice, soaked for ½ hour
½ cup shelled green peas	3 tablespoons oil

2 bay leaves	1 teaspoon cumin seeds
4-5 black peppercorns	1 medium onion, sliced
2 green chillies, slit	1 large potato, peeled and diced
2-4 green cardamoms	Salt to taste
4 cloves	

1. Heat the oil in a deep non-stick pan. Add the bay leaves, peppercorns, green chillies, cardamoms, cloves and cumin seeds and sauté till fragrant. Add the onion and sauté till translucent.
2. Add the crushed nuggets, potato and green peas and cook for two to three minutes. Add four cups of water and salt.
3. Drain the rice and add. Stir lightly and once the mixture comes to a boil, cover and cook on low heat for ten minutes.
4. Place the pan over a heated tawa and cook for four to five minutes or till the rice is done. Serve hot.

Pyaaz aur Pudine ki Roti

- 2 medium onions, finely chopped
- 1 cup finely chopped fresh mint
- 2 cups whole-wheat flour
- Salt to taste
- 2 green chillies, chopped
- ½ teaspoon carom seeds
- 1 teaspoon dried pomegranate seeds, roasted and crushed
- Oil, as required

1. Place the flour and salt in a deep bowl. Add the onions, fresh mint, green chillies, carom seeds and dried pomegranate seeds and knead into a stiff dough with enough water. Cover with a damp cloth and let it rest for twenty to twenty five minutes.
2. Divide the dough into eight equal portions. Shape them into balls. Roll out each ball into a medium-sized roti.
3. Heat a non-stick tawa, place one roti at a time on it, and cook for half a minute. Flip it over, apply a little oil on it, and flip it again. Apply a little oil on the other side too. Cook turning sides till both sides are light golden. Serve hot.

Spicy Pinwheels

1 unsliced bread loaf

6 tablespoons sandwich spread

6 tablespoons Chhunda (page 12)

1. Slice the bread horizontally into four slices. Remove the crusts from all the sides.
2. Place each bread slice on the worktop. Spread one and a half tablespoons of sandwich spread and one and a half tablespoons of chhunda evenly on it.
3. Roll up each bread slice and wrap it up tightly in a cling film. Refrigerate the rolls for fifteen to twenty minutes.
4. Cut the bread roll into one-inch thick round slices and serve immediately.

Chef's Note You can replace the chhunda with any spicy chutney.

Spicy Pinwheels
French Toast

Idli Fry
Spicy Moong Dal Dhokla

Idli Fry

16 leftover idlis, quartered	2 green chillies, slit
2 tablespoons oil + for deep-frying	2 medium onions, chopped
1 teaspoon mustard seeds	½ teaspoon turmeric powder
1 teaspoon cumin seeds	¼ teaspoon red chilli powder
10-12 curry leaves	Salt to taste
A pinch of asafoetida	4 tablespoons chopped fresh coriander

1. Heat sufficient oil in a kadai and deep-fry the idli till crisp. Drain on absorbent paper and set aside.
2. Heat two tablespoons of oil in a non-stick pan. Add the mustard seeds and cumin seeds. When the seeds start spluttering, add the curry leaves, asafoetida, green chillies, onions and sauté till the onions become translucent.

3. Add the turmeric powder, chilli powder, salt and idli and mix well. Sprinkle some water, cover and cook for four to five minutes.
4. Serve hot, garnished with the chopped coriander.

Spicy Moong Dal Dhokla

1 cup skinless split green gram, soaked

2-3 green chillies

2 tablespoons chopped fresh fenugreek

2 teaspoons gram flour

2 pinches of asafoetida

¼ teaspoon fruit salt

2 pinches of sugar

2 teaspoons + 1 tablespoon oil + for greasing

Salt to taste

½ teaspoon mustard seeds

10-12 curry leaves

1. Blend the soaked green gram in a blender with the green chillies and a little water. Transfer into a bowl. Add the fresh fenugreek, gram flour, one pinch of asafoetida, fruit salt, sugar, two teaspoons oil, salt and mix well to make a thick batter.
2. Pour into a greased thali and steam in a steamer for about twenty minutes. Remove, cool slightly and cut into pieces.
3. Heat one tablespoon of oil in a small non-stick pan. Add the mustard seeds, curry leaves, and the remaining asafoetida. Mix and pour over the dhokla. Serve hot with Green Chutney (page 94).

(Image on page 60)

Dal Dhokli

1 cup split pigeon peas, soaked	¾ teaspoon turmeric powder
¾ cup whole-wheat flour	¾ teaspoon red chilli powder
¼ cup gram flour	2 pinches of asafoetida
Salt to taste	2 tablespoons oil

1½ tablespoons peanuts
2 tablespoons pure ghee
¾ teaspoon mustard seeds
¼ teaspoon fenugreek seeds
2 dried red chillies, broken
10 curry leaves
1½ teaspoons green chilli paste
1 teaspoon grated jaggery
1 tablespoon lemon juice
2 tablespoons chopped fresh coriander
1 small onion, finely chopped

1. Mix the whole-wheat flour and gram flour in a bowl. Add the salt, one-fourth teaspoon turmeric powder, chilli powder, a pinch of asafoetida, half tablespoon of oil and sufficient water to knead into a stiff dough.
2. Boil the split pigeon peas in a deep non-stick pan with two cups of water, salt and the remaining turmeric powder. Add the peanuts when half done. Continue to cook till completely cooked. Whisk the mixture till smooth.
3. Divide the dough into equal portions and roll out each portion into thin roti, apply a little oil on either side. Cut into diamond shapes. Set aside.
4. Heat half the ghee in another deep non-stick pan. Add the mustard seeds, fenugreek seeds, a pinch of asafoetida, red chillies, curry leaves and green chilli paste.

5. When the seeds splutter, add the cooked dal and mix. Add two cups of water. When the mixture starts boiling, add the jaggery. When the jaggery dissolves, add the dough strips and cook, stirring occasionally, so that the dough strips do not stick to the bottom of the vessel. Adjust the salt.
6. Once the dough strips are cooked take the pan off the heat. Add the lemon juice and mix. Serve in individual bowls, garnished with the chopped coriander and onion. Drizzle a little ghee, if desired.

Fansi Dhokli

300 grams French beans, chopped
2 tablespoons oil
½ teaspoon mustard seeds
½ teaspoon cumin seeds
½ teaspoon carom seeds
A pinch of asafoetida
Salt to taste
½ teaspoon turmeric powder
½ teaspoon red chilli powder
2 teaspoons coriander-cumin powder
1 teaspoon sugar
2 teaspoons lemon juice
1 tablespoon chopped fresh coriander

Dhokli

¼ cup gram flour

1 tablespoon whole-wheat flour

¼ teaspoon red chilli powder

¼ teaspoon turmeric powder

A pinch of asafoetida

2 teaspoons oil

Salt to taste

1. To make the dhokli, combine gram flour, whole-wheat flour, chilli powder, turmeric powder, asafoetida, oil and salt; add water as required and knead into a semi-soft dough. Shape into a ball and then roll out into an eight-inch disc. Cut into diamonds. Cover and set aside.

2. Heat the oil in a deep non-stick pan and add the mustard seeds. As they begin to splutter add the cumin seeds, carom seeds, and asafoetida. Add the French beans and mix well. Add the salt, turmeric powder, chilli powder, coriander-cumin powder and one cup of water and mix well. Cover and cook, on low heat, till the beans are nearly done.

3. Add half a cup of water and bring it to a boil. Add the dhokli and stir gently. Cover and cook on low heat for ten to twelve minutes, stirring at regular intervals, till the dhokli is cooked. Add the sugar and lemon juice and mix well. Serve hot, garnished with the chopped coriander.

Chef's Note Fansi is the Gujarati word for French beans.

Rajma Cheese Parantha

1/3 cup kidney beans, soaked overnight

2 cups grated cheese

4 cups whole-wheat flour

1 medium onion, chopped

2-3 green chillies, chopped

1 teaspoon chopped fresh coriander

1 teaspoon coriander seeds

1 teaspoon red chilli powder

½ teaspoon dried pomegranate seeds, crushed

8-10 fresh mint, finely chopped

Salt to taste

½ teaspoon dried mango powder

Oil, as required

1. Drain and pressure-cook kidney beans in one cup of water till pressure is released four to five times (four to five whistles).
2. Cool, strain and reserve the liquid and mash the kidney beans.

3. Mix the flour, onion, green chillies, chopped fresh coriander, coriander seeds, kidney beans, chilli powder, dried pomegranate seeds, fresh mint, and salt in a deep bowl.
4. Add the required amount of reserved cooking liquid and knead into a soft and pliable dough. Cover with a damp cloth and rest it for fifteen minutes.
5. To make the stuffing, mix the cheese, dried mango powder and salt in a bowl.
6. Divide the dough into eight equal portions and shape them into balls. Shape each ball into a katori ensuring that the edges are thinner than the centre.
7. Place a portion of the cheese mixture in it. Shape again into a ball and roll out into a thick parantha.
8. Heat a non-stick tawa, brush a little oil on it and place a parantha on it.
9. Cook on medium heat for half a minute on each side. Lower heat and cook till both the sides are slightly brown. Serve hot.

Rajma Cheese Parantha

Spicy Red Mexican Rice

Spicy Red Mexican Rice

2 cups cooked rice
2 tablespoons oil
¾ teaspoon carom seeds
2 medium onions, finely chopped
4 tablespoons tomato purée
1 tablespoon tomato ketchup
1 medium green capsicum, chopped
1 teaspoon red chilli powder
Salt to taste
½ teaspoon crushed black peppercorns
3-4 tablespoons chopped fresh coriander

1. Heat the oil in a non-stick pan. Add the carom seeds and onions and sauté till the onions turn light brown.
2. Add the tomato purée and cook for two minutes, then add the tomato ketchup, capsicum, chilli powder, salt and crushed peppercorns.
3. Add the rice and gently stir-fry for two to three minutes. Add the chopped coriander and mix well. Serve hot.

Chana Dal Halwa

- 1½ cups split Bengal gram, soaked for 2 hours and cooked
- 2 tablespoons ghee
- 20 cashew nuts
- 2 tablespoons raisins
- ½ cup desiccated coconut
- 3 tablespoons poppy seeds
- 4-5 cloves
- 2 cups grated jaggery

1. Heat the ghee in a non-stick pan. Add the cashew nuts and sauté till golden brown. Drain on absorbent paper and set aside.
2. In the same pan, add the raisins and sauté for a minute. Drain on absorbent paper and set aside. Grind together the coconut and poppy seeds to a fine powder.
3. Add the cloves and cooked Bengal gram to the same pan. Add four cups of water, the ground powder and mix well. Cook till the mixture comes to a boil.
4. Add the jaggery and keep stirring till it melts. Serve hot, garnished with the cashew nuts and raisins.

Palak Methi Puri

½ cup fresh spinach purée
½ cup chopped fresh fenugreek
1½ cups whole-wheat flour
1 teaspoon ginger-green chilli paste
Salt to taste
1 tablespoon oil + for deep-frying

1. Combine together the flour, spinach purée, fenugreek leaves, ginger-green chilli paste, salt and one tablespoon of oil and knead into a firm dough. Cover it with a damp cloth and rest the dough for about ten minutes.
2. Divide the dough into sixteen equal portions and shape into balls. Roll out each into four-inch round puri.
3. Heat sufficient oil in a kadai and deep-fry the puri, one by one, on medium heat.
4. Drain on absorbent paper and serve hot.

Bajre ke Bharwan Paranthe

¾ cup millet flour, sifted

¾ cup sifted whole-wheat flour + for dusting

Salt to taste

8 teaspoons roasted sesame seeds

Ghee for shallow-frying

Stuffing

2 medium unripe bananas

Salt to taste

2 green chillies, chopped

1 teaspoon Chaat Masala (page 94)

½ teaspoon red chilli powder

½ teaspoon Garam Masala Powder (page 94)

1 teaspoon chopped fresh coriander

1. Steam the bananas in their skins in a steamer for seven to eight minutes. Peel them while hot and put them in a bowl and mash.

2. Add the salt, green chillies, chaat masala, red chilli powder, garam masala powder and chopped coriander, and mix well. Divide into four equal portions and set aside.
3. Mix the millet flour, whole-wheat flour, salt with sufficient water and knead into a soft dough. Divide into four equal portions and roll into balls.
4. Sprinkle some whole-wheat flour on the worktop. Place each ball and spread gently with fingertips, taking care that the outer edges are thinner than the centre.
5. Place a portion of the stuffing in the centre, gather the edges together and seal. Roll into a ball again. Ensure that the stuffing is totally enclosed in the dough.
6. Spread the sesame seeds on a plate and press each ball lightly in it on one side only. Roll each of them in whole-wheat flour and place on the floured worktop. Gently pat each ball once again to as thin a parantha as you can.
7. Heat a non-stick tawa and lightly grease it. Place each parantha on it, one at a time, and cook for half a minute. Flip it over, drizzle some ghee all around and cook. Flip again, drizzle some more ghee all around and cook till both sides are light golden.
8. Serve hot.

Hara Bhara Paneer

250 grams cottage cheese, cut into ½-inch cubes

1 large bunch (500 grams) fresh spinach leaves, trimmed

3 teaspoons oil

1 inch ginger, finely chopped

6-8 garlic cloves, chopped

3 green chillies, chopped

1 medium onion, chopped

¼ teaspoon turmeric powder

½ cup yogurt, whisked

2 teaspoons powdered dried fenugreek leaves

Salt to taste

2 tablespoons fresh cream

1. Boil four cups of water in a deep non-stick pan.
2. Add the spinach leaves and blanch for thirty to forty seconds. Drain and immerse in iced water.
3. Drain again and blend into a smooth purée.

4. Heat the oil in a deep non-stick pan. Add the ginger, garlic, and green chillies and sauté for thirty seconds.
5. Add the onion and sauté till golden brown. Add the turmeric powder and sauté. Add the yogurt and mix well. Cook till the oil separates.
6. Add the spinach purée and mix well. Add the dried fenugreek leaves and salt. Mix well. Add the cottage cheese cubes and mix lightly. Add the fresh cream and mix well. Serve hot.

Sweetcorn and Capsicum Stir-Fry

1 cup sweetcorn kernels, boiled	2 medium onions, chopped
2 medium capsicums, chopped	2 medium tomatoes, chopped
3 tablespoons oil	1 teaspoon ginger-garlic paste

½ teaspoon turmeric powder

¾ teaspoon red chilli powder

Salt to taste

¼ teaspoon sugar

1 teaspoon Garam Masala Powder (page 94)

2 tablespoons fresh cream

1 inch ginger, cut into thin strips

1. Heat the oil in a non-stick kadai, add the onions and sauté till it turns a light brown.
2. Add the tomatoes and sauté for three to four minutes. Add the ginger-garlic paste and sauté for a minute.
3. Add the capsicums and cook for two to three minutes.
4. Add the turmeric powder, chilli powder, salt, and sweetcorn. Mix and cook till the oil begins to separate from the masala.
5. Add the sugar, garam masala powder and cream and stir well.
6. Garnish with the ginger strips and serve hot with phulke.

Papad Koshimbir

6 masala papad, roasted
1 small onion, finely chopped
1 medium tomato, finely chopped
1 green chilli, finely chopped
2 tablespoons freshly grated coconut
2 teaspoons lemon juice
¼ teaspoon red chilli powder
Chaat Masala (page 94), to taste
Salt to taste
2 tablespoons finely chopped fresh coriander

1. Combine the onion, tomato, green chilli and coconut in a bowl and mix well.
2. Add the lemon juice, chilli powder, chaat masala and salt and mix again. Crush the papad and add. Mix gently.
3. Serve immediately, garnished with the chopped coriander.

Carrot Methi Sabzi

4 medium carrots, chopped

1 medium bunch (350 grams) fresh fenugreek, chopped

2 tablespoons oil

1 medium onion, chopped

½ teaspoon green chilli-ginger paste

3 garlic cloves, minced

½ teaspoon turmeric powder

Salt to taste

1 tablespoon coriander-cumin powder

1 teaspoon lemon juice

1. Heat the oil in a non-stick kadai. Add the onion and sauté till light brown.
2. Add the green chilli-ginger paste and garlic and sauté for half a minute. Add the carrots and fenugreek and mix well.
3. Add the turmeric powder and salt. Mix well, cover and cook on low heat, stirring occasionally, till the carrots are done. Add the coriander-cumin powder and lemon juice and mix well. Serve hot with chapati.

Kurkuri Ajwaini Bhindi

3 tablespoons carom seeds
250 grams ladies' fingers
3 tablespoons gram flour
3 tablespoons rice flour
Oil for deep-frying

Masala

1½ teaspoons Chaat Masala (page 94)
1 teaspoon red chilli powder
Salt to taste

1. Trim the two ends of the ladies' fingers and slice diagonally. Transfer into a bowl.
2. Add the gram flour, rice flour, and carom seeds and toss once. Sprinkle a little water so that the flours nicely coat the ladies' fingers and toss again.
3. To make the masala, mix the chaat masala, chilli powder, and salt in a bowl.
4. Heat sufficient oil in a kadai. Deep-fry the ladies' fingers in small batches, on medium heat, till golden and crispy. Drain on absorbent paper. Sprinkle the masala on top and mix well. Serve immediately.

Pressure-Cooked Aloo Sabzi

- 6 medium potatoes, cut into cubes
- 2 tablespoons oil
- ½ teaspoon mustard seeds
- ½ teaspoon cumin seeds
- A pinch of asafoetida
- 7-8 curry leaves
- 2 large tomatoes, finely chopped
- ½ teaspoon turmeric powder
- Salt to taste
- 1 teaspoon red chilli powder
- 1 teaspoon coriander-cumin powder
- 2 teaspoons chopped fresh coriander
- ½ teaspoon Garam Masala Powder (page 94)

1. Heat the oil in a pressure cooker; add the mustard seeds.
2. When they splutter, add the cumin seeds. When the cumin seeds begin to change colour, add the asafoetida, curry leaves, tomatoes, turmeric powder and salt.
3. Mix well and sauté till tomatoes are soft.

4. Add the chilli powder and coriander-cumin powder. Mix well and sauté for a minute. Add the potatoes and three-fourth cup of water. Mix well and bring to a boil.
5. Cover the cooker with the lid and cook under pressure till pressure is released three times (three whistles). Open the lid of the cooker after the pressure reduces completely, sprinkle the chopped coriander and garam masala powder. Serve hot with chapati or thepla.

Hare Moong ki Chhaaswali Khichdi

¾ cup whole green gram, soaked for 3-4 hours

4 cups buttermilk

½ cup rice, soaked for ½ hour and drained

1 teaspoon ghee

1 teaspoon cumin seeds

4-5 cloves

2 medium carrots, cut into 1-inch pieces

4-6 cauliflower florets, cut into small pieces

3-4 green chillies, slit

½ teaspoon turmeric powder

Salt to taste

2 tablespoons chopped fresh coriander

1. Heat the ghee in a pressure cooker. Add the cumin seeds and cloves and sauté for a minute.
2. Add the carrots, cauliflower, green gram, green chillies, turmeric powder and rice and mix well. Add the buttermilk and salt. Add the chopped coriander and mix well. Cover the cooker with the lid and cook under pressure till pressure is released twice (two whistles).
3. Lower the heat and cook for eight to ten minutes more. Remove from heat. Open the lid of the cooker when pressure reduces completely. Serve hot.

Bhein Masala

2 lotus stems (7 inches each), cleaned and scraped
3 tablespoons oil
1 inch ginger, chopped
2-3 green chillies, chopped
1 teaspoon cumin seeds
1 medium onion, finely chopped
2 medium tomatoes, finely chopped
Salt to taste
¾ teaspoon turmeric powder

1 teaspoon red chilli powder

2 teaspoons coriander powder

3 medium potatoes, cut into cubes

1 teaspoon Garam Masala Powder (page 94)

1 tablespoon chopped fresh coriander

1. Slice the lotus stems into thin round slices.
2. Heat the oil in a pressure cooker; add the ginger and green chillies and sauté for a few seconds. Add the cumin seeds and as they begin to change colour, add the onion. Sauté till it begins to change colour. Add the tomatoes and mix well.
3. Add the salt, turmeric powder, chilli powder and coriander powder and sauté till oil separates from the masala. Add the lotus stem slices and potatoes and mix well. Add one and half cups of water and bring to a boil. Cover the cooker and cook under pressure till the pressure is released four to five times (four to five whistles).
4. Open the cooker after the pressure reduces completely. Place back on heat and cook till the moisture dries and the masala coats the lotus slices thickly.
5. Sprinkle the garam masala powder and mix. Add the chopped coriander and stir. Serve hot with roti.

Tender Coconut and Sago Kheer

1 cup chopped tender coconut
½ cup sago, soaked
¾ cup grated palm jaggery
½ teaspoon green cardamom powder
3 cups coconut milk
10-12 pistachios, finely chopped
10-12 almonds, finely chopped

1. Heat two cups of water in a non-stick handi. Add the sago and cook on low heat for ten to twelve minutes or till the sago gets cooked.
2. Add the palm jaggery and cardamom powder and stir on low heat till the jaggery dissolves completely. Add the coconut milk and mix. Cook for two to three minutes. Add the tender coconut, half the pistachios and almonds and mix. Stir and cook for five to seven minutes or till the kheer thickens.
3. Transfer into a serving bowl, decorate with the remaining pistachios and almonds and serve.

Chef's Note Make sure that the kheer is not too thick.

Quick Trifle
Tender Coconut and Sago Kheer

Nariyal ka Halwa

Nariyal ka Halwa

1 cup grated fresh coconut

2 tablespoons ghee

½ cup sugar

2 tablespoons milk

A few saffron threads, soaked in 1 tablespoon warm milk

¼ teaspoon green cardamom powder

10-12 chopped pistachios, for decoration

1. Heat the ghee in a non-stick kadai. Add the coconut and sauté for two to three minutes.
2. Add the sugar and milk and mix well. Cover the kadai and cook on low heat for four to five minutes. Uncover, stir once, and continue to cook till the sugar dissolves.
3. Mix in the saffron-flavoured milk and cardamom powder.
4. Decorate with the pistachios. Serve hot.

Quick Trifle

250 grams chocolate sponge cake
1 can (500 grams) chopped mixed fruits with syrup
1 cup whipped cream
2 tablespoons chopped dark chocolate

1. Halve the sponge cake horizontally. Place one half in a glass bowl and drizzle two tablespoons of the fruit syrup over it.
2. Spread half the whipped cream over the cake and sprinkle three-fourth cup chopped mixed fruits.
3. Cover with the other half of the sponge cake and spread the remaining whipped cream over it. Sprinkle the remaining chopped mixed fruits over the cream.
4. Sprinkle the chocolate on top and refrigerate for one hour.
5. Cut into wedges and serve chilled.

(Image on page 87)

Sooji aur Badam ka Halwa

¼ cup coarse semolina, roasted
1 cup almonds
3 tablespoons pure ghee
¾ cups sugar
1 cup milk
A few saffron threads
¼ teaspoon green cardamom powder

1. Dry-roast the almonds in a non-stick pan. Cut eight to ten almonds into slivers for garnishing and coarsely powder the rest.
2. Heat the ghee in a non-stick kadai and sauté the semolina till light brown. Add the almond powder and continue to sauté for two or three minutes.
3. Add the sugar, milk, half cup water and saffron and mix. Cook over medium heat, stirring continuously, till the sugar dissolves and the mixture attains the consistency of halwa. Add the cardamom powder and mix well.
4. Remove from heat, decorate with slivers of the reserved almonds and serve hot.

Mango Cheesecake

Crust

8-10 bran biscuits or digestive biscuits

4 tablespoons butter, melted

Filling

2 cups mango pulp

½ teaspoon mango essence

1 cup milk

½ cup condensed milk

1 tablespoon cornflour

1 tablespoon unflavoured gelatine

1½ cups drained yogurt

2 cups cottage cheese

½ cup sugar, powdered

Topping

1 tablespoon mango jelly crystals

1 mango, chopped

1. Crush the biscuits to a coarse powder and place it in a bowl. Add the butter and mix well. Place the mixture at the base of a six-inch round spring-form tin lined with greaseproof paper. Press the mixture down lightly and place it in the refrigerator to set.

2. For the filling, heat the milk in a non-stick pan. Add the condensed milk and mix. Mix the cornflour with a little milk and add it to the hot milk. Cook, stirring continuously, till the mixture thickens. Set aside.
3. Mix the gelatine in a little water in a bowl and heat it in the microwave for one minute. Remove and set aside.
4. Place the drained yogurt in a bowl. Add the cottage cheese and whisk well. Add the mango pulp and mix again. Add the mango essence and the milk mixture and mix again. Add the powdered sugar and blend the mixture with a hand blender. Add the dissolved gelatine and blend again.
5. Pour the mixture into the prepared tin over the biscuit layer. Refrigerate for two to three hours. In a pan, dissolve the mango jelly crystals in a quarter cup of water. Bring to a boil, remove from heat and set aside to cool. Spread a layer of mango jelly over the set cheesecake. Chill until the jelly sets.
6. Remove from the spring-form tin and cut into eight wedges with a sharp knife dipped in hot water. Serve chilled, decorated with the chopped mango.

Chef's Note: A spring-form tin is a round shallow cake tin with a removable base.

Basic recipes

Chaat Masala

Dry-roast 4 tablespoons coriander seeds, 2 teaspoons cumin seeds and 1 teaspoon carom seeds separately. Cool and powder them with 2-3 whole dried red chillies, 3 tablespoons black salt and ½ teaspoon citric acid. Mix in 1 teaspoon dried mango powder, 1 tablespoon salt and 1 teaspoon white/black pepper powder. Store in an airtight container.

Green Chutney

Grind together 1 cup fresh coriander, ½ cup fresh mint, 2-3 green chillies, black salt to taste, ¼ teaspoon sugar and 1 tablespoon lemon juice to a smooth paste using a little water if required.

Garam Masala Powder

Dry-roast 10-12 blades mace, 8-10 one-inch cinnamon sticks, 25 cloves, 25 green cardamoms, 10-12 black cardamoms, 2 whole nutmegs, 8-10 bay leaves, 8 teaspoons cumin seeds and 4 teaspoons black peppercorns separately, on a tawa. Cool and grind together all the spices to a fine powder. Store in an airtight jar in a cool, dry place.

Makes 100 grams of garam masala powder.

Tamarind Pulp

Soak 75 grams tamarind in 100 ml warm water for 10-15 minutes. Grind to a smooth paste and strain to remove any fibres. Store in an airtight container in the refrigerator.

Glossary

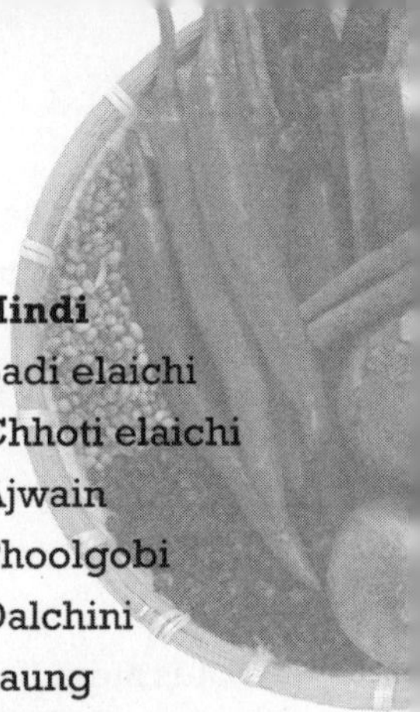

English	Hindi
Almonds	Badam
Amaranth leaves	Choulai bhaji
Bay leaf	Tej patta
Bean sprouts moong	Ankurit
Bengal gram, split	Chana dal
Bitter gourds	Karela
Black gram, skinless, split	Dhuli urad dal
Bottle gourd	Doodhi
Brown gram	Matki/moth
Buttermilk	Chhaas
Cabbage	Pattagobi
Capsicum	Shimla mirch
Cardamoms, black	Badi elaichi
Cardamoms, green	Chhoti elaichi
Carom seeds	Ajwain
Cauliflower	Phoolgobi
Cinnamon	Dalchini
Cloves	Laung
Cluster beans	Gavarphalli
Coriander seeds	Dhania
Cumin seeds	Jeera
Dried fenugreek leaves	Kasuri methi
Dried mango powder	Amchur
Dried Pomegranate seeds	Anardana
Drumstick	Saijan ki phalli

English	Hindi
Fenugreek seeds	Methi dana
Fenugreek, fresh	Methi dana
Gram flour	Besan
Green gram, skinless, split	Dhuli moong dal
Jaggery	Gur
Kidney beans	Rajma
Ladies' finger	Bhindi
Lotus stem	Bhein
Millet	Bajra
Mushroom	Khumb
Nutmeg	Jaiphal
Peppercorns	Kali mirch
Pigeon peas, split	Tuvar dal/ arhar dal

English	Hindi
Pine nuts	Chilgoze
Pistachios	Pista
Poppy seeds	Khuslhus
Raisins	Kishmish
Refined flour	Maida
Saffron	Kesar
Sago	Sabudana
Semolina	Sooji/rawa
Sesame seeds	Til
Spinach	Palak
Tamarind	Imli
Vermicelli	Seviyan
Yogurt	Dahi
Yogurt, hung (drained)	Chakka